READ ABOUT IT
Activities for Teaching Basic Reading Skills
Primary

Imogene Forte

Thank You

to Mary Catherine Mahoney
and to Elaine Raphael
editors
to Dennas Davis
cover designer
and especially to Mary Hamilton
artist and wordsmith

Library of Congress Catalog Card Number 82-80499
ISBN 0-86530-006-2

These Adventures In Reading Belong To

If you can catch the Unicorn
And mount it for a ride,
You'll find that hidden, secret worlds
Appear before your eyes.

You'll meet with gnomes and goblins
Fauns and fairies, friends and foes.
No dreamy realm of fantasy
Is very far from home.

You'll walk the land of giants those
In fearsome forests lie.
The Unicorn will take you there
And never leave your side.

So ride away the Unicorn,
To know the world that was,
The world the way it is today,
Or what is yet to come.

Adventure lasts a lifetime if
You're willing to pursue
Each newly opened book to bring
The Unicorn to you!

ABOUT THIS BOOK

READ ABOUT IT was written to provide interesting, fun-filled pages to help boys and girls achieve reading independence. The activities have been carefully designed to reinforce and extend vocabulary and comprehension skills. Easy-to-follow directions, fanciful fantasy-based themes, and the use of a controlled but not limited vocabulary encourage purposeful reading.

To simplify classroom or home use, the reproducible skills-based activity pages have been organized into two broad areas:

I. Word recognition and usage
   A. Phonetic analysis
   B. Structural analysis
   C. Word meaning
   D. Word sensitivity

II. Independent reading skills
   A. Comprehension
   B. Work/study
   C. Library and reference materials
   D. Rate, accuracy, and appreciation

Each of the worksheets is designed to stand alone and to present one complete reading experience. They may be used to supplement and reinforce adopted textbooks and courses of study and are appropriate for use in either individual or group settings. For classroom use, teachers will want to review the skills as listed in the table of contents and plan the order and manner of presentation to meet student needs. In a home or other setting where the book is used individually, the pages will fall into a natural skills sequence and can be used most efficiently in the order presented.

The purposes of this collection of read-think-and-do pencil and paper activities, puzzles, games, and fun projects are to encourage kids to stretch their minds, develop their imaginations, and enjoy the thrill of successful personal reading.

Come, let's READ ABOUT IT!

Imogene Forte

TABLE OF CONTENTS

WORD RECOGNITION AND USAGE
SKILLS

If you can catch the Unicorn
And mount it for a ride,
You'll find that hidden, secret worlds
Appear before your eyes.

THE MAGIC E

The Good Vowel Fairy has left this magic "E" wand for Binky Bunny.

Binky wants to change all her short-vowel words to long-vowel words.

Read the directions to help Binky finish her homework.

not _____   mad _____

hug _____   us _____

cap _____   tub _____

bit _____   hop _____

cub _____   hid _____

at _____   cut _____

hat _____

can _____

Dear Binky,
Add an E to each short-vowel word to make it a long-vowel word.
love,
The Good
Vowel Fairy

PICK A PICTURE

Look at the pictures in the boxes.

Circle any picture whose name does not start with the letter in that box.

Color the other pictures.

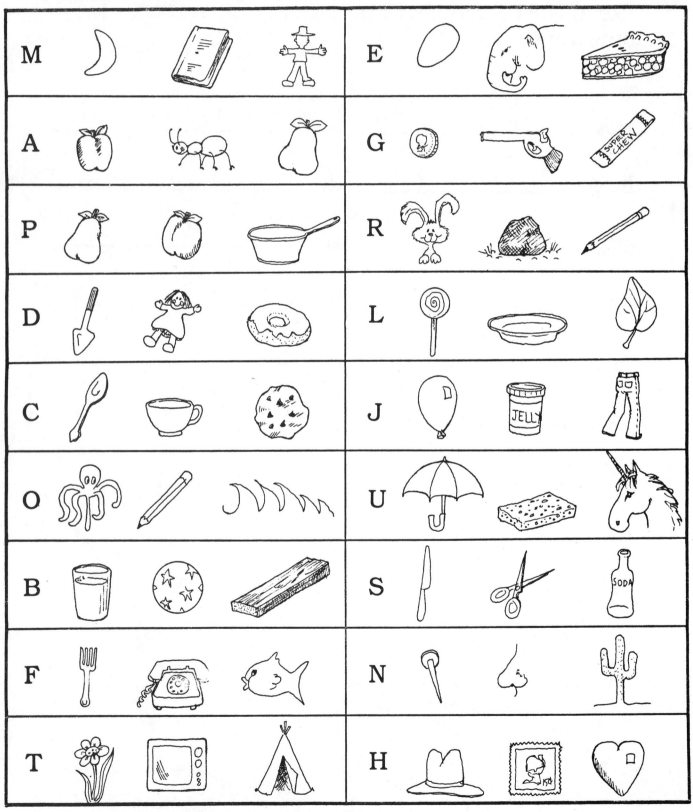

A SPLENDID SPIDER WEB

Spinky Spider is spinning a special spider web. This splendid spider web must be filled with words beginning with the consonant blend "sp-."

Find and circle 21 words in the word-find box. Words appear up and down or across.
Write the words in Spinky Spider's web.

W	A	S	P	A	D	E	N	S	E	D	O
U	S	P	E	A	K	I	S	P	U	N	E
F	E	I	S	P	O	O	N	A	L	T	D
I	S	N	O	H	S	P	S	R	A	M	I
S	P	E	L	L	P	S	P	R	I	N	G
P	U	D	O	E	I	P	I	O	T	F	S
R	R	S	E	S	R	O	D	W	A	R	P
E	T	P	S	P	I	K	E	F	O	R	E
A	L	O	P	I	T	E	R	S	T	O	N
D	U	K	I	C	O	N	S	P	E	E	D
E	V	E	L	E	S	P	O	U	T	N	O
T	I	E	L	O	S	P	I	N	A	R	D

SLY BLENDS

Circle nine things in this picture that begin with the consonant blend "gr-."

Underline ten things in this picture that begin with the consonant blend "st-."

A FUNNY PHONICS FLOWER GARDEN

Color all the consonant spaces purple.
Color all the vowel spaces red.
How many funny phonics flowers did you color? ____

RHYME FIND

Finish these rhymes.

Words to use:

car
post
bell
bike
sky
cat

I saw a ghost
Right next to that _____ !

My sister's _____
Is awfully fat!

He put a guitar
In the trunk of his _____ .

Please ring the_____
If you find a shell.

I wish that I
Could touch the _____ .

If you don't want to hike,
You may ride your _____ .

RHYME LINE

Put a word on the line
To make your own rhyme!

The poor little bug
Got caught in a

_____.

There once was a man
Whose house was a

_____.

One night in a tree
All the owls drank

_____.

Old Freddie the frog
He just likes to

_____.

Jack's the only crow I know
Who likes to stand out in the

_____.

I got a phone call from a hen
Who talked to me 'til almost

_____.

STAR LIGHT, STAR BRIGHT

To solve the puzzle and find the hidden picture, read the phrases below and follow the directions.

1. If **clock** rhymes with **block,** color the #1 spaces.
2. If **star** rhymes with **bar,** color the #2 spaces.
3. If **sky** rhymes with **shed,** color the #3 spaces.
4. If **night** rhymes with **nine,** color the #4 spaces.
5. If **mid** rhymes with **map,** color the #5 spaces.
6. If **moon** rhymes with **spoon,** color the #6 spaces.
7. If **bright** rhymes with **fright,** color the #7 spaces.
8. If **dark** rhymes with **look,** color the #8 spaces.
9. If **cloud** rhymes with **count,** color the #9 spaces.

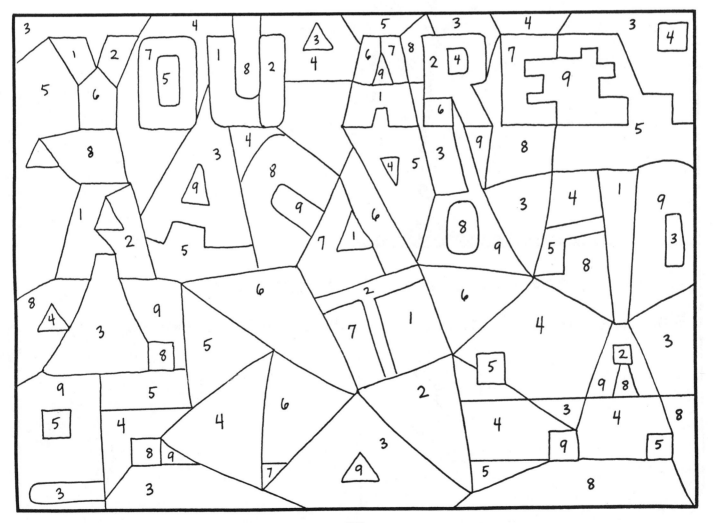

MYSTERY MOUNTAIN

A storm on Mystery Mountain has scrambled up the syllables in these words.

Rearrange the syllables correctly to find out what the sentences say.

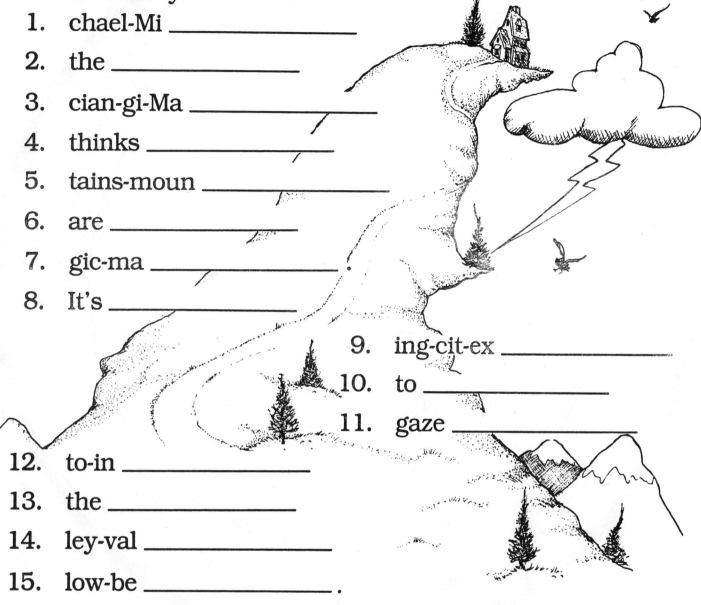

1. chael-Mi _____

2. the _____

3. cian-gi-Ma _____

4. thinks _____

5. tains-moun _____

6. are _____

7. gic-ma _____.

8. It's _____

9. ing-cit-ex _____

10. to _____

11. gaze _____

12. to-in _____

13. the _____

14. ley-val _____

15. low-be _____.

Add 3 sentences of your own to tell more about Michael the Magician.

_____

_____

_____

21

PREFIX GO-ROUND

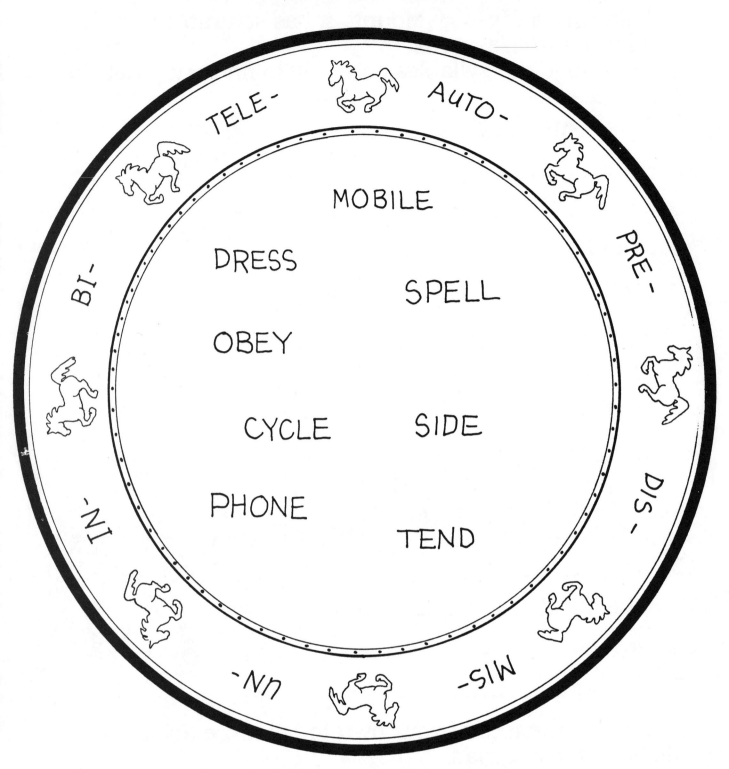

Draw a line from each prefix on the Prefix Wheel to a word in the center of the wheel to make new words.

22

MAGICIAN'S MAKEOVER

Marlowe the Magician is busy "making over" words by adding suffixes to root words to form new words.
Draw a line from each suffix on the "suffix line" to a word in the box below to make a new word.

ON TARGET

Anhu wants to become a great hunter.
Every day he practices with his bow and arrows.
You can help Anhu with his target practice.
The letter targets he is shooting at are two words of which contractions can be made.
Draw an apostrophe arrow (′) through the letters to be left out to form a contraction.
Write the contraction under the target.

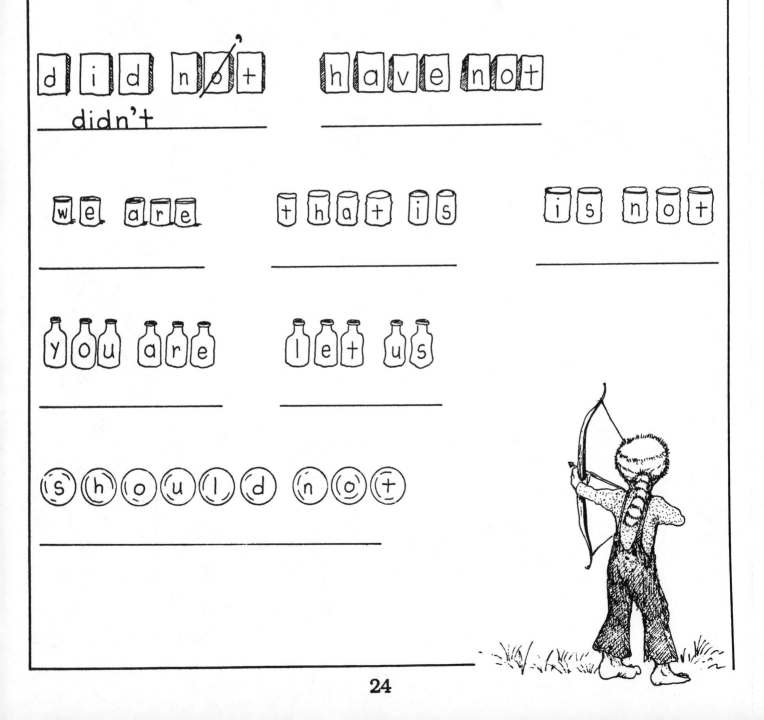

did n̸o̸t   have not

__didn't__   _____

we are   that is   is not

_____   _____   _____

you are   let us

_____   _____

should not

_____

WRITE FOR WILLIE

Willie Worm forgot all about his homework.
Now he is in real trouble.
Maybe you can help him out.
First read his word list.
Then write the correct abbreviation beside each term.

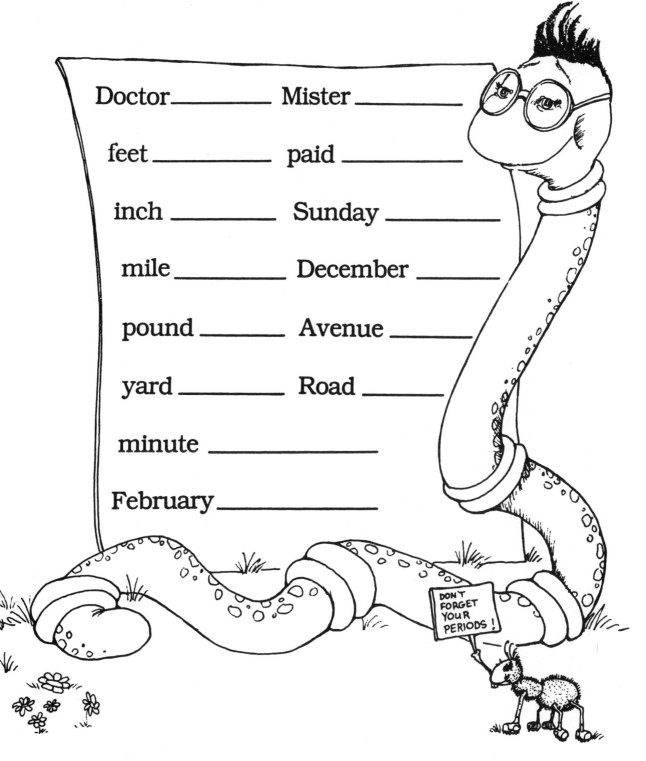

Doctor _____ Mister _____

feet _____ paid _____

inch _____ Sunday _____

mile _____ December _____

pound _____ Avenue _____

yard _____ Road _____

minute _____

February _____

DON'T FORGET YOUR PERIODS!

25

COMPOUND TOP

Round and round goes the Compound Top!
Circle the words to make it stop!

Find and circle 19 compound words on the top.

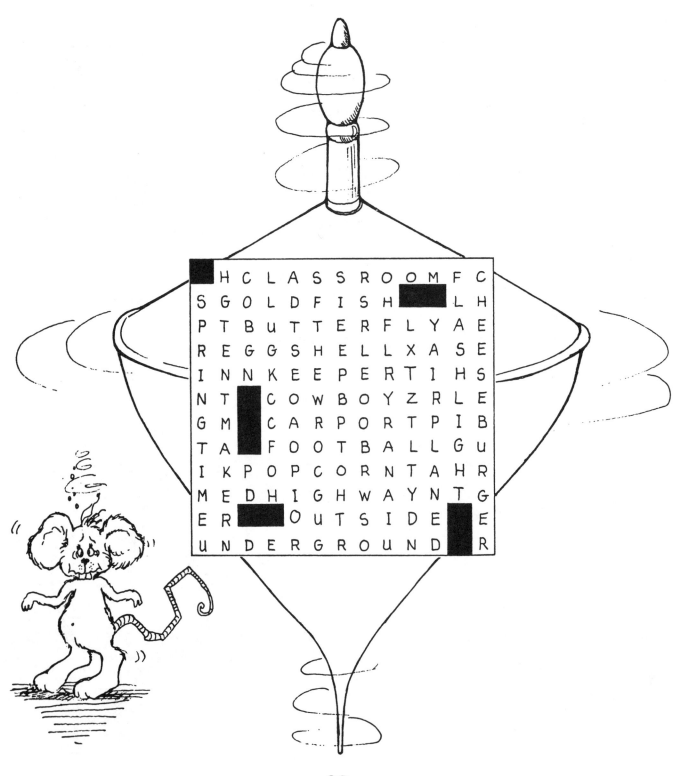

PICK THE PLURALS

"Pick" the flower in each group that shows <u>more than one</u>, and circle it.

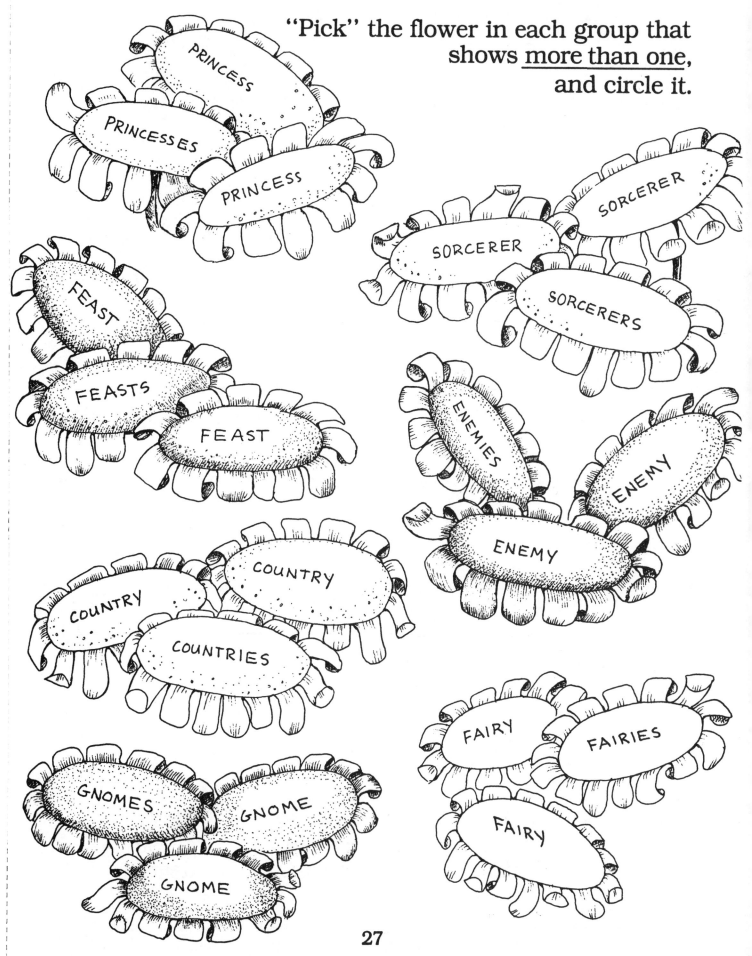

27

TWO BY TWO
Old Noah built his ark . . .

When Noah built his ark
He brought the creatures in
Two by two.

Write the correct plural words from the list at the bottom of the page to complete Noah's passenger list.

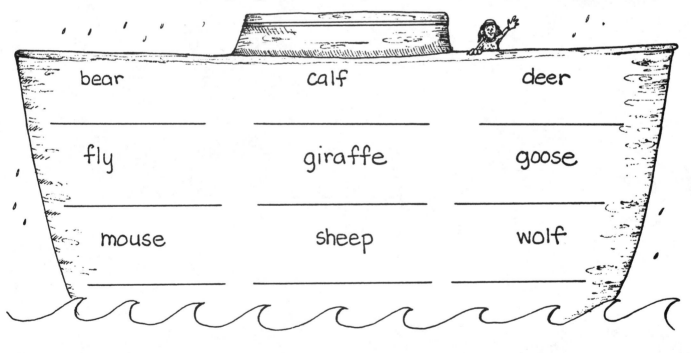

bear	calf	deer
_____	_____	_____
fly	giraffe	goose
_____	_____	_____
mouse	sheep	wolf
_____	_____	_____

Plurals: calves   wolves   flies
          giraffes sheep   geese
          mice   bears   deer

FAMILY FUN

Write a word to finish each sentence below.
Figure out what words you need by looking at this picture.

Words to use:

father	line	ball	Grand	mower

1. _____ mother is reading to Joey.
2. Mother is pushing the lawn _____ .
3. Father is hanging wet towels on the clothes
    _____ .
4. Ethel and Arnold are tossing a base _____ .
5. Grand _____ is bringing lemonade for
    everyone.

KING WISEAPPLE'S REBUS

Old King Wiseapple's wizard got stuck in one of his own magic spells and disappeared before he could solve these two rebuses. If you can solve them, you can become King Wiseapple's new wizard!

Look at the rebus boxes and figure them out. Write your solution on the line below each rebus block.

T + 👶 + L, T + 👶 + L, L + 🧤 − M + L ⭐

1. _____

H + 🐂 − C 👁 1 + 🚪 W + 🎩 U R.

1. _____

✳ B N + 🪡 − TH, ✳ B Qu + 😖 − S

2. _____

✳ J + 😣 − L O + 4 THE 🕯 + 🌿

2. _____

THE DWARF

Read the story below and fill in each blank with the proper word from the word list.

Rain was falling as the _____ little dwarf hurried down the narrow street as _____ as his _____ legs would carry him. He moved _____ from doorway to doorway, hoping he would not be _____ . Under the plain brown cloak that covered his _____ little body, he carried a _____ bundle of great value.

At last he came to the cottage of a _____ farmer just outside the village. He very carefully laid the bundle on the doorstep, rapped _____ on the door, and hurried away before he could be seen. When the farmer and his wife opened the door, they saw only the bundle lying on the step. Seeing what it was, the woman snatched it up and cried with tears of _____ , "Oh, blessings on the kind and _____ soul who has rescued our _____ baby from the castle of the wicked queen. Surely the queen was jealous of the beauty of our child and took him for her own. Whoever has returned him to us is a noble person indeed!"

Word list:

twisted	joy	spindly
ugly	noticed	beautiful
quickly	secret	brave
loudly	poor	quietly

31

PACK THE BASKET

Hooray! Today is Picnic Day at Gnome Glen.
Help the gnomes get ready for it.
Mark out the item in each group that does not
belong at a picnic.

32

MACK NEEDS HELP

Mack needs help.
The fruits and vegetables are all mixed up.
Mark out the word in each basket that does not belong.

THE LEPRECHAUN'S MUSIC BOX

There are 20 words hiding in the leprechaun's music box.

Read the list of words.

Then find and circle them in the music box.

Words to find:

music	record	band	jazz
pop	singer	hum	beat
notes	piano	time	song
melody	tape	chorus	rhythm
drum	guitar	radio	clap

```
T I M E P O H U M O
A F I P S I N G E R
P I A N O N A U L H
E S B A N D E I O Y
T O N P G U J T D T
C H O R U S A A Y H
W P T A C E D R U M
O Y E D B L O E K P
M U S I C J A Z Z F
R E C O R D N P O E
```

HOMONYM HOMEWORK

Help Patricia Pixie finish her homework by writing the correct homonym in the space beside each word. (You will find all the homonyms hiding in the word box!)

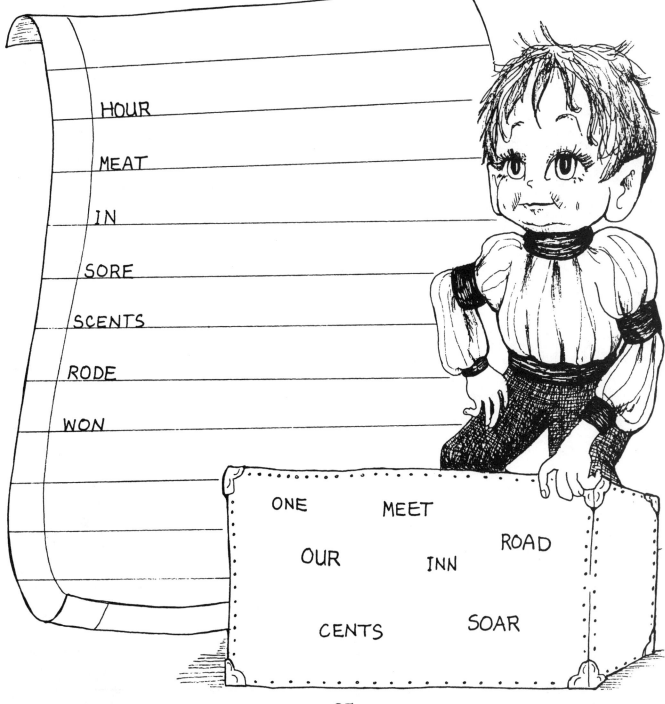

HOUR

MEAT

IN

SORE

SCENTS

RODE

WON

ONE   MEET

OUR   INN   ROAD

CENTS   SOAR

ROYAL WORDS

In each group below, cross out the word that does not belong.

Write a sentence explaining why it does not belong.

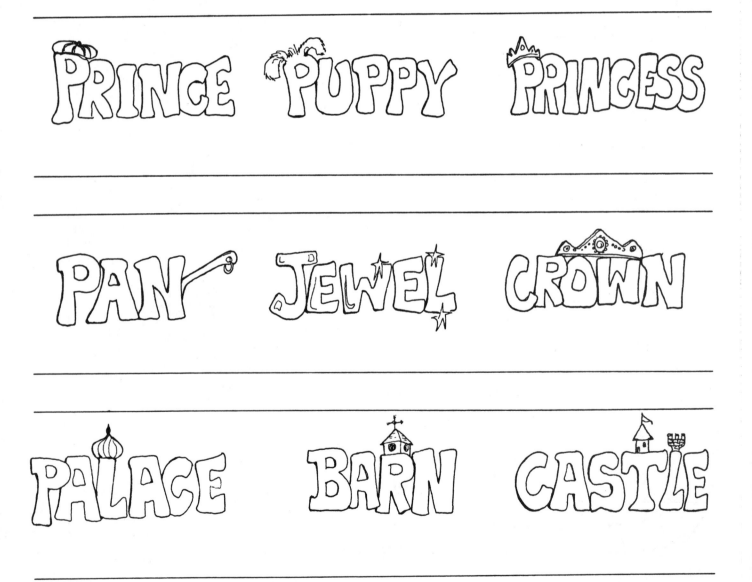

KING   QUEEN   NURSE

PRINCE   PUPPY   PRINCESS

PAN   JEWEL   CROWN

PALACE   BARN   CASTLE

GOBLINS

AND

HOBGOBLINS

GOBLIN

HOBGOBLIN

Fill each blank below with the best descriptive word from this list.

Words to use:
troublesome   friendly   frighten   exciting
interesting   harmless   terrifying   mean

1. Goblins are said to be bad-hearted and
_____ creatures.

2. Goblins are pictured as little, ugly and
_____ .

3. Goblins like to torment and _____
their victims.

4. Meeting a goblin would be a _____
experience for most people.

5. Hobgoblins are believed to be_____
spirits who do only mischievous deeds.

6. Hobgoblins are _____ little
creatures who like to play tricks on people.

7. Getting acquainted with a hobgoblin might be
_____ and_____ .

PICTURE THE MEANING

Draw a picture to illustrate the meaning of each saying below.

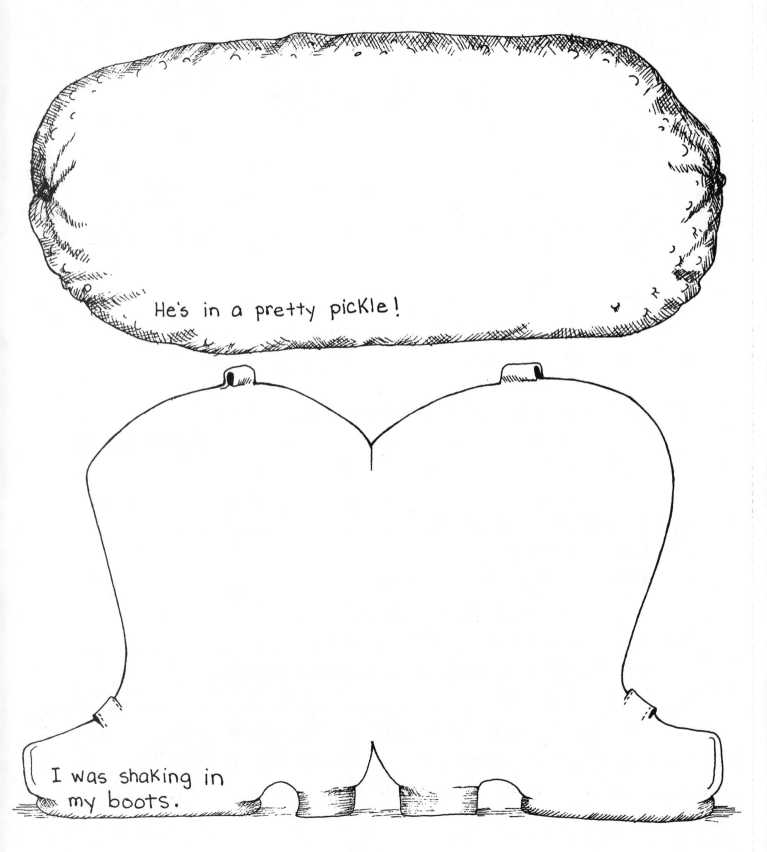

He's in a pretty pickle!

I was shaking in my boots.

A SCARY TRAIL

To find your way out of the haunted house, follow the scary word trail. Write a word from the word list to finish each sentence.

Words to use:

afraid   scared   frightened
alarmed   terrified   insecure

WHEN A CAR I AM RIDING IN STARTS TO SKID ON THE STREET, I AM

_____.

WHEN SOMEONE TELLS ME A GHOST STORY, I AM

_____.

WHEN A STRAY DOG STARTS TO CHASE MY BIKE, I AM

_____.

WHEN EVERYONE IN MY CLASS UNDERSTANDS A JOKE, I FEEL EXCEPT ME

_____.

When I smell smoke coming from the hall-way, I am

_____.

When I hear strange noises in the middle of the night, I am

_____.

START

QUICK-ESCAPE!

WISH YOU WERE HERE

Take a good look at this ugly monster.

Pretend that you can jump into the picture and walk right up to him. (He's really very friendly!)

Once you are there, answer the questions below.

1.   If you shook hands with the monster, his hand would feel

_____ .

2.   If he leaned over very close to you, his breath would smell

_____ .

3.   If he asked you to scratch his back, it would feel

_____ .

4.   When he spoke to you, his voice would sound like

_____ .

5.   If he opened his mouth to yawn, you would see his teeth were _____ .

6.   If he started to chase you, you would run very

_____ .

OFF TO BATTLE

Look at the picture carefully.
Select a word from the list below to finish each sentence.

Words to use:
    dangerous   brave   frightening   grouchy

1. The dog looks _____ .

2. The _____ troll is falling behind.

3. The dark sky is_____ .

4. These soldiers need to be _____ .

WHICH IS WHAT?

Look carefully at the 3 characters below.
On the lines next to each picture, write the 4 words
from the word list which best describe that creature.

Words to use:
beautiful
cruel
harmless
magical
noble
playful
quick
scary
strong
tiny
ugly
wicked

WITCH

_____

_____

_____

_____

Unicorn

_____

_____

_____

_____

Elf

_____

_____

_____

_____

A BAG OF WORDS

Use your dictionary to find words to describe this creature.

Try to fill the bag.

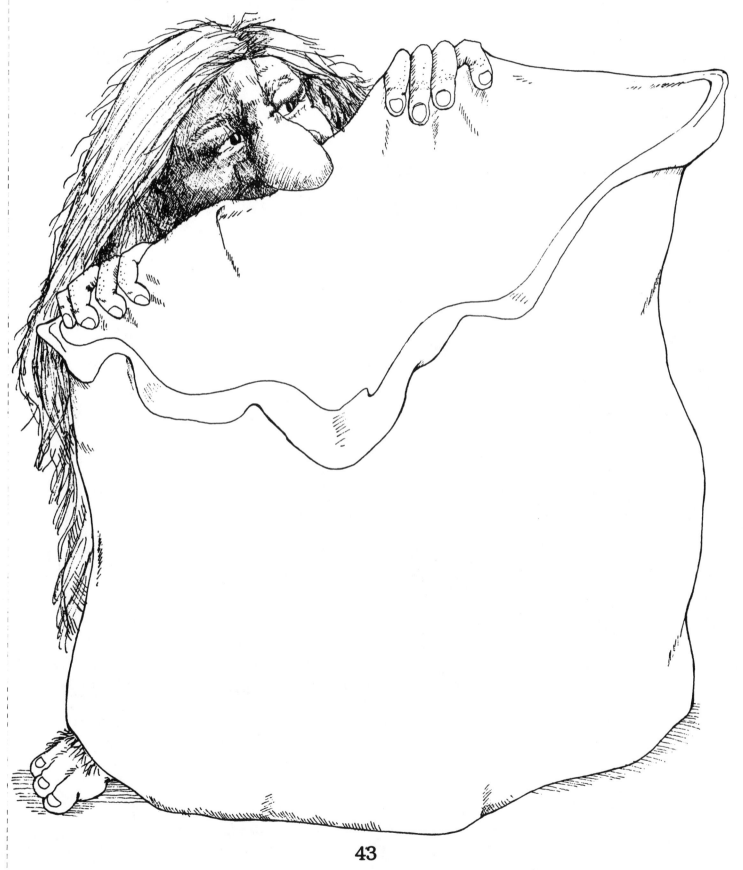

GOODIES FOR A GNOME

Fill the gnome's basket with goodies! Write food
words on the shapes. Begin each food name with the
last letter of the name of the food touching it.

Words to use:

grapes   egg   apple   milk   ham   squash

WORD-MAKER, WORD-MAKER!!

Look at each word in the word packages below.

Make 6 new words from each word by changing 1 letter at a time. The first one is done for you.

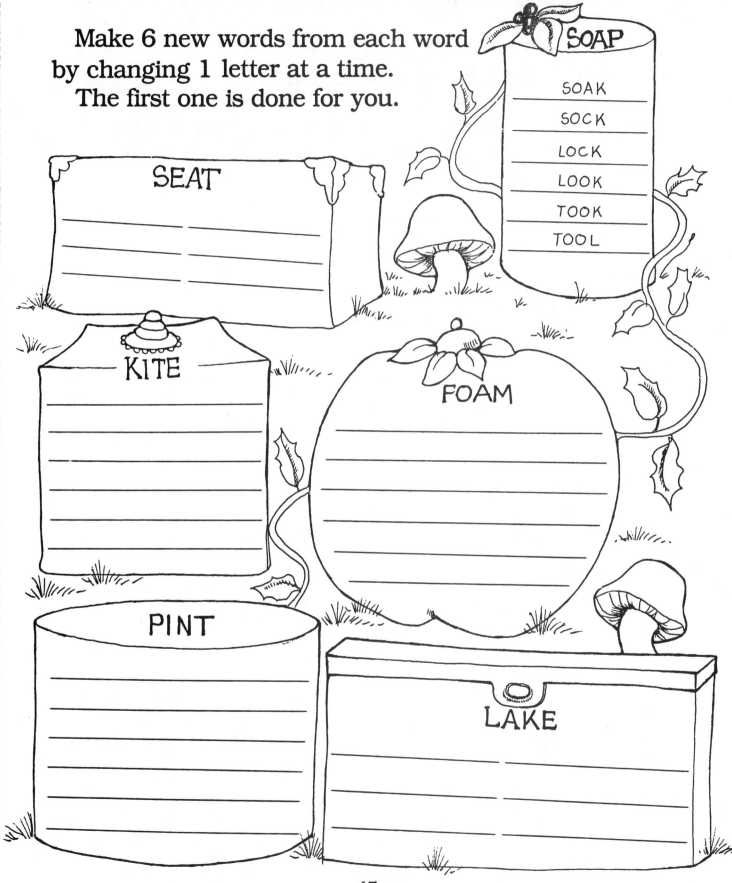

SOAP

SOAK
SOCK
LOCK
LOOK
TOOK
TOOL

SEAT

KITE

FOAM

PINT

LAKE

THE MAGIC TRIANGLE TANGLE

Morto the Magician has to use his magic wand to find 25 words that can be made from the letters in this word:

T R I A N G L E S

You can do it with just your pencil!

Write the 25 words you find on the lines below.

Notes: Each word must be at least 4 letters long.

No letter may be used more than 1 time in a word.

GET OUT OF THE JUNGLE

Find your way out of the jungle by crossing out every other letter on the path, beginning with the second letter.

Write the names of the jungle animals as you meet them.

START → E D L S E U P G H B A C N

1. _____

2. _____

3. _____

4. _____

5. _____

6. _____

7. _____

NO DICTIONARY, PLEASE

Select any one letter of the alphabet. Without using a dictionary, try to write 30 words that begin with the letter.

1. _____
2. _____
3. _____
4. _____
5. _____
6. _____
7. _____
8. _____
9. _____
10. _____
11. _____
12. _____
13. _____
14. _____
15. _____
16. _____
17. _____
18. _____
19. _____
20. _____
21. _____
22. _____
23. _____
24. _____
25. _____
26. _____
27. _____
28. _____
29. _____
30. _____

It would be fun to ask a friend to do this with you. Using the same letter, race to see who can write 30 words first.

48

HOW'S YOUR WORD KNOWLEDGE?

Read this story carefully.
Then answer the questions below.

1. One day in the middle of our trip, we agreed to go sightseeing.
2. We split into 3 groups and decided to meet at the car at 5:00.
3. At 3:00 p.m. I had already forgotten where the car was.
4. "Let's see if we can find the car," I said to my older brother.
5. We walked around until we saw familiar sights.
6. "It's just around this corner," my brother said.
7. "I know — great!" I said.
8. We turned the corner, but the car wasn't there.
9. "Has the car disappeared or are we lost?" I asked.

1. Circle the word that best could be used to take the place of **agreed** in sentence 1.

    decided   argued   thought

2. Circle the word that means almost the same thing as **split** in sentence 2.

    divided   joined   remained

3. Circle the word that means the opposite of **forgotten** as it is used in sentence 3.

    guessed   slipped   remembered

4. Circle the phrase that best explains what **familiar** means in sentence 5.

    we had seen them before
    we never had seen them
    we didn't know whether we had seen them

5. Circle the word that explains how the person who is telling the story feels at the end.

    happy   confused   hungry

INDEPENDENT READING

SKILLS

So ride away the Unicorn
To know the world that was,
The world the way it is today,
Or what is yet to come.

ELVES AT WORK

Study this picture for a few minutes.
Then cover the picture with a sheet of paper.

Complete the sentences.
Then uncover the picture to check your answers.

1. There are _____ elves in the picture.

2. The smallest elf has a _____ in his hand.

3. The basket is filled with _____ .

4. The elf with a crooked hat is _____ .

5. The table is set for _____ people.

6. A good title for this picture would be

_____ .

KAHLIL THE SHEPHERD

Read the story below.
Underline the topic sentence in each paragraph.

Late one afternoon, Kahlil the shepherd sat watching his flock. It was his job to care for the sheep of the village. Each day, he would take the flock out to graze. Each day, he and his faithful dog Ali would look after them, keeping the wolves away and helping the little lambs that got caught in the bushes. Today they had been very busy, and now everything was quiet and calm.

Suddenly Ali started to bark and growl. Kahlil jumped up and looked around to see what had made Ali angry. He saw nothing, but he heard a "clip, clop, clip, clop." It sounded like a horse coming slowly up the road. He looked down the path and saw an old man walking, leading a tired donkey behind him. The old man looked so sad and the donkey so thin that Kahlil felt sorry for them.

When they reached Kahlil, he nodded and said, "Old man, you look tired and hungry, and so does your donkey. Stop here and rest for a moment. I'll share my bread and cheese with you and your donkey may graze with my sheep, if you will tell me the tale of your journey. I have never left this village, and I would like to hear about the wide world. Your looks say you have seen much of it."

BOOK RECORD

1. Title: _____

   Author: _____

2. Number of pages: _____

3. This book is about _____

   _____

   _____

   _____

4. New words I want to know about:

   _____   _____   _____

   _____   _____   _____

   _____   _____   _____

5. Date I started this book: _____

   Date I finished this book: _____

6. Compared to other books I have read, this book is _____

   _____

THE OLD LADY AND THE FAIRY

Read the story below.
Circle and label the words in each sentence that tell
who, what, when, where, why, and **how.**
Be careful! All the sentences do not tell all these
things.

One winter morning, a kind old lady sat shivering
beside her small fire, trying to keep warm.

Suddenly a fairy appeared before her. The fairy said,
"By my magic, I am here now to grant you one wish."

"Oh, good fairy," cried the old woman, "with your
magic, make it warm now in my house so I will not
freeze to death." Right away, because the fairy waved
her magic wand, the house became warm and cozy.

"I thank you very much for your kindness to me this
day," said the old woman.

The fairy smiled, gave the
old lady a kiss on the
forehead, and instantly
disappeared.

THE CRYSTAL BALL

Look into the crystal ball.
Find the word that completes each sentence.
Write each word in the correct blank.

1. _____ is to **fairy** as **staff** is to **wizard.**

2. _____ is to **queen** as **pointed hat** is to **witch.**

3. **Sing** is to **bird** as _____ is to **toad.**

4. _____ is to a **bad witch** as **white magic** is to a **good witch.**

5. _____ is to a **princess** as **stomping** is to an **ogre.**

6. A _____ is to a **witch** as a **horse** is to a **knight.**

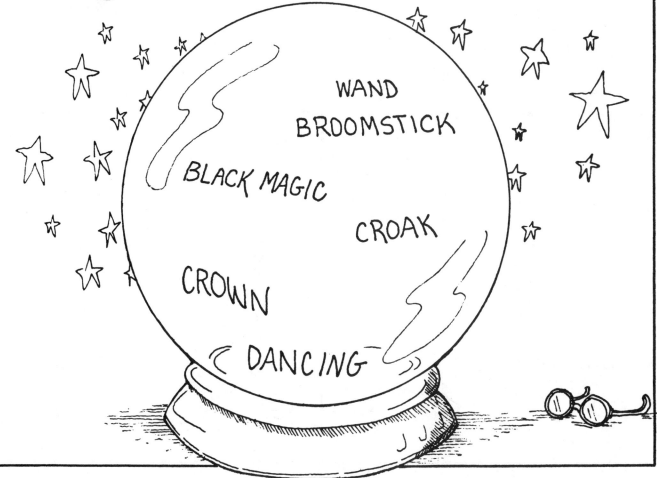

WAND
BROOMSTICK
BLACK MAGIC
CROAK
CROWN
DANCING

57

WHAT GOES WHEN?

This comic strip is out of order.
Read and cut out each frame.
Put the frames in order.
Write the correct number (1-4) on each.
Color the pictures.

A SPRING STORM

Elvira and her family were taking a driving trip across the country.

As they drove one day, Elvira asked her mom to turn on the radio so they could listen to some music. Just as her mom tuned in a station, this newscast came on.

This is station WKZR in Bean Blossom. Our newsroom has just received information that a freak spring snowstorm is moving into our territory from the northwest at 37 miles per hour, and should reach Bean Blossom within an hour. All schools and daycare centers are sending their students home now before the storm hits. All businesses are closing. High winds of up to 45 miles per hour, blowing snow and sleet will accompany the storm and will cause limited visibility and bad driving conditions.

The storm is expected to last until noon tomorrow. Stay tuned to station WKZR in Bean Blossom for further information on the storm as it develops. In the meantime, get home and stay warm!

Underline only the most important facts in the above newscast. Then using only the facts, rewrite the bulletin in as few words as possible.

_____

_____

_____

_____

_____

AFTER MOTHER GOOSE

Underline each word in the Mother Goose rhymes that tells what the main character did.

Draw a picture to show what you think happened next.

Old King Cole
Was a merry old soul,
And a merry old soul was he.
He called for his pipe,
And he called for his bowl,
And he called for his fiddlers three!

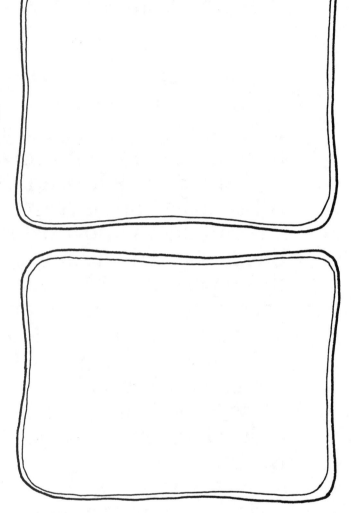

Little Miss Muffet
Sat on a tuffet
Eating her curds and whey.
Along came a spider
And sat down beside her
And frightened Miss Muffet away.

Little Jack Horner
Sat in a corner,
Eating a Christmas pie.
He stuck in his thumb
And pulled out a plum,
And said, "What a good boy am I!"

ROYAL CONCLUSIONS

Finish the following diagrams by drawing picture conclusions in the spaces provided.

CHANGE THE STORY

All summer long, the grasshopper danced and sang in the warm sunshine. When winter came and the earth was bare, there was nothing for him to eat.

One cold day, the hungry grasshopper saw an ant happily eating dinner. "Where did you get that lovely food?" he asked.

"Oh," said the ant, "I always store food in the summer so I will have something to eat in the winter."

"Will you please give me just enough to keep me from starving?" begged the grasshopper.

"No, I won't," said the ant. "You danced and sang all summer while I worked. Now you can just dance and sing all winter!"

Write what you think would have happened if ...

1. The ant had kindly invited the grasshopper for some food.

_____

_____

_____

_____

_____

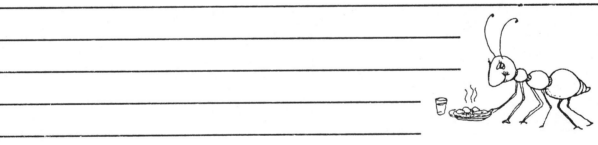

2. The grasshopper had been a thief and had tried to rob the ant.

_____

_____

_____

_____

FAR-OUT FACTS

Read this ad from the Galaxia *Gazette,* then answer the questions below.

At last, hair that is
OUT OF THIS WORLD!!!

If you have wanted to try the new "Solar-shock" look that is sweeping the galaxy, **MOONDRIPS** shampoo is just for you! Even fine, limp hair can be made to stand on end with this wonderful shampoo. Made with tiny bits of magnet, **MOONDRIPS** will keep your new hairdo charged with life for days!

Only $3.95 per bottle.

MOONDRIPS
SHAMPOO

Sold only at the Star-Struck Store.

1. What is the ad trying to sell? _____

2. What is this product made from that makes it special? _____

3. What kind of hair does it especially work on? _____

4. In what store can it be found? _____

5. How much does the product cost? _____

IT'S A FACT!

Some of the sentences below state facts. That means they are true.

Some of the sentences state opinions. That means they are what someone thinks, and are not necessarily true.

Circle the sentences that state facts. Underline the sentences that state opinions.

1. I think Roberto will win the race today.

2. There are 9 planets in our solar system.

3. The month of January has 31 days.

4. An omelet is made from eggs.

5. I think I hear footsteps outside my window.

6. Angela is the best skater in the world.

7. Monster stories are the best ones to read.

8. There are 7 days in a week.

9. Swimming is more fun than any other sport.

10. A period goes at the end of a "telling" sentence.

BECAUSE OF THE WEATHER

Read the sentences below.
Choose the correct word to finish each sentence.
Write the words in the correct spaces.

Words to use:

melt	dangerous	closed
excitement	happy	slowly

The first snowstorm of the season filled the town

with _____ .

By midnight, the roads will be _____ .

Because of the storm, schools will be _____ .

The school holiday will make the children

_____ .

Buses and cars will move through the snow

_____ .

Tomorrow, the sunshine will cause

the snow to _____ .

COLORFUL CHARACTERS

Underline the words and phrases in each sentence that tell you something about the character of that person.

1. The wicked witch looked slyly around as she sat waiting for the children.

2. Bonjo, the happy jester, always tried to make people laugh.

3. The new page in the castle tiptoed timidly into the throne room and meekly found his place.

4. Princess Angelina always laughed gleefully and called happily to people on the street as she drove by in the royal coach.

5. Even though Ingle was just a tiny elf, he spent his time planning mean tricks and jokes to play on people.

WHAT DOES IT LOOK LIKE?

Sometimes when you say a word, you can see exactly what you think it looks like in your mind. For instance, when you say the word "pumpkin," you might see it like this.

Read the following words. Draw a picture of each as you "see" it in your mind.

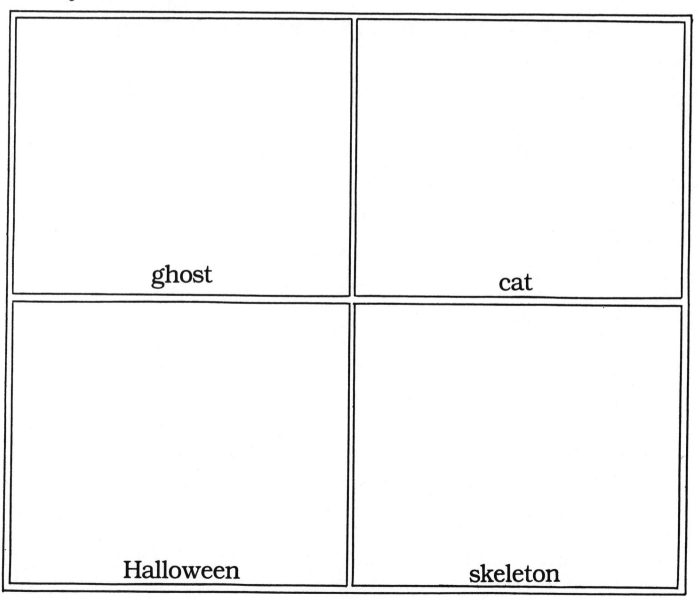

ghost

cat

Halloween

skeleton

A B C BAKERY

Help Mr. Edwards arrange his new bakery.
Place the items on each shelf in alphabetical order by
writing them on the lines below the shelf.

Muffins: bran; corn; blueberry
Doughnuts: maple; cream-filled; jelly
Pies: pecan; pumpkin; apple
Cakes: carrot; devil's food; coconut

Cookies: peanut butter; sugar;
chocolate chip
Bread: rye; wheat; raisin

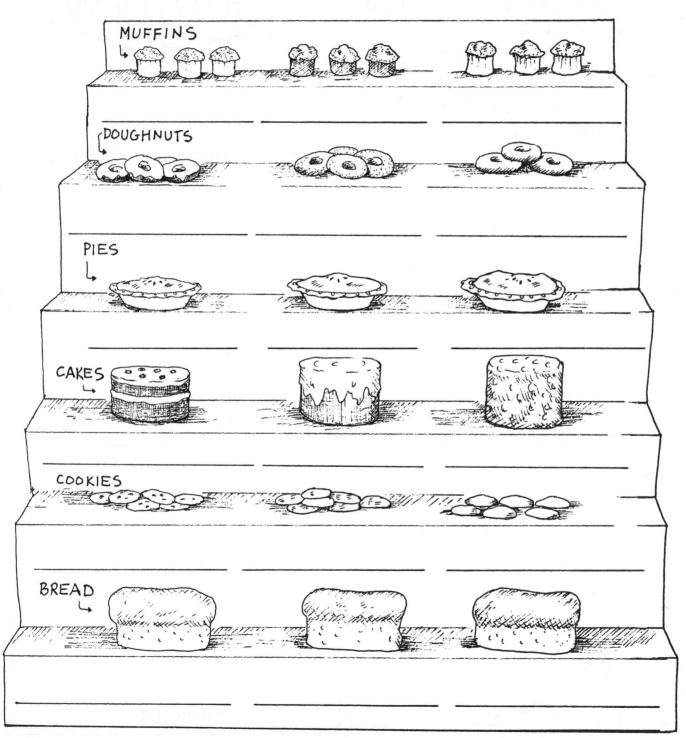

LAWS OF THE LIBRARY

Unscramble the sentences to find 3 rules for using your library.

Recopy each rule onto one of the bookmarks. Color and cut out the bookmarks to use in your favorite books.

books they Return due are before or renew.

_____

many on Read subjects books different.

_____

library are things Learn in where the.

_____

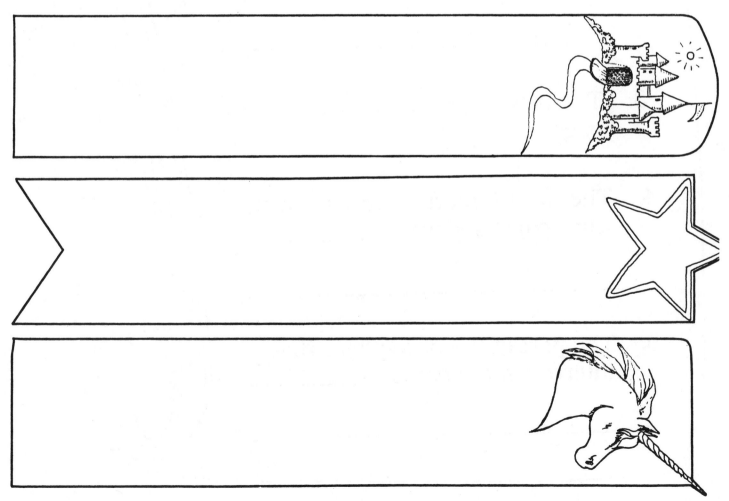

KNOW YOUR NEWSPAPER

Use a copy of today's newspaper to complete the sentences below.

- SPORTS
- TV
- COMICS

YOUR OWN

Hometown News

TODAY'S PAPER

$.25

1. The full name of the newspaper is

   _____ .

2. The newspaper is dated

   _____ .

3. The newspaper has _____ pages.

4. The most important article on the front page is about _____

   _____ .

5. The part of the newspaper that interests me most is _____

   _____ .

AFTER THE RAIN

Use red, green, yellow, purple, gold and blue
To color this picture — a secret just for you!

Color the #1 spaces red.
Color the #2 spaces green.
Color the #3 spaces yellow.
Color the #4 spaces purple.

Color the #5 spaces blue.
Color the #6 spaces gold.

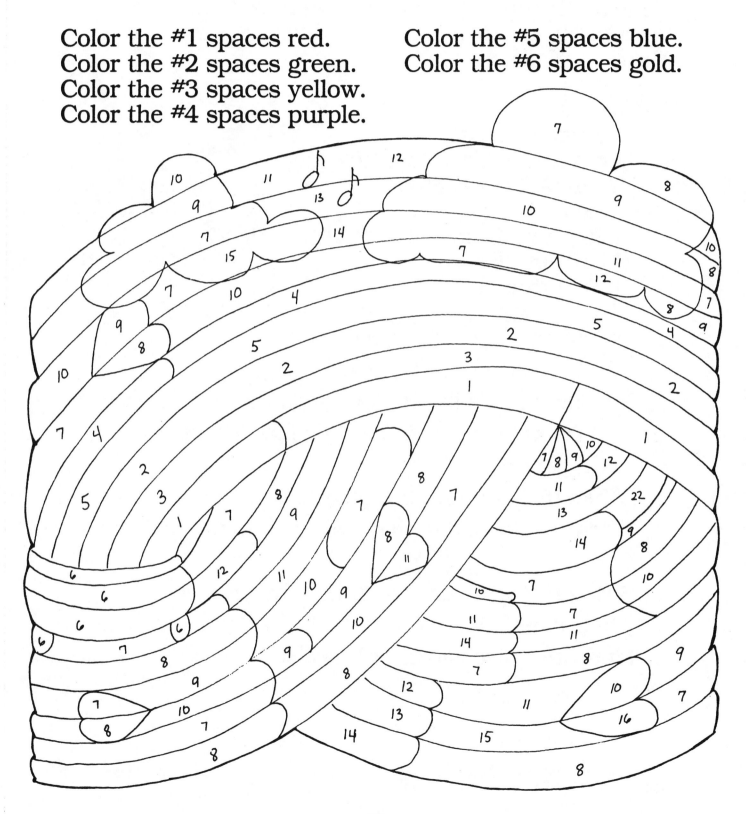

JEWELRY FIT FOR A WITCH

The chief designer for the witches' jewelry factory had a bad day.

The instructions for making spooky seed jewelry are mixed up.

Read all the instructions, then number them in the correct order in which they should take place.

Hurry — Halloween is on its way!

What to use:
> pumpkin seeds
> orange and black food coloring
> 2 small jars with tops
> water
> paper towels or newspapers
> heavy needle
> heavy thread

_____ Spread the seeds on paper to dry.

_____ Add ½ teaspoon of water to each jar.

_____ Put some seeds in each of 2 jars. Put a little orange food coloring in one jar; a little black food coloring in the other jar.

_____ Shake the jars until the seeds are colored.

_____ Wash the pumpkin seeds. Spread them on paper to dry.

_____ String the seeds in several lengths to make witches' jewelry. You can make original, one-of-a-kind rings, necklaces, or bracelets.

Adapted from Puddles & Wings & Grapevine Swings by Imogene Forte and Marjorie Frank. Copyright 1982 by Incentive Publications, Inc. Used by permission.

THE ENCHANTED VALLEY

Follow the directions below to break the spell and bring life back to the enchanted valley.

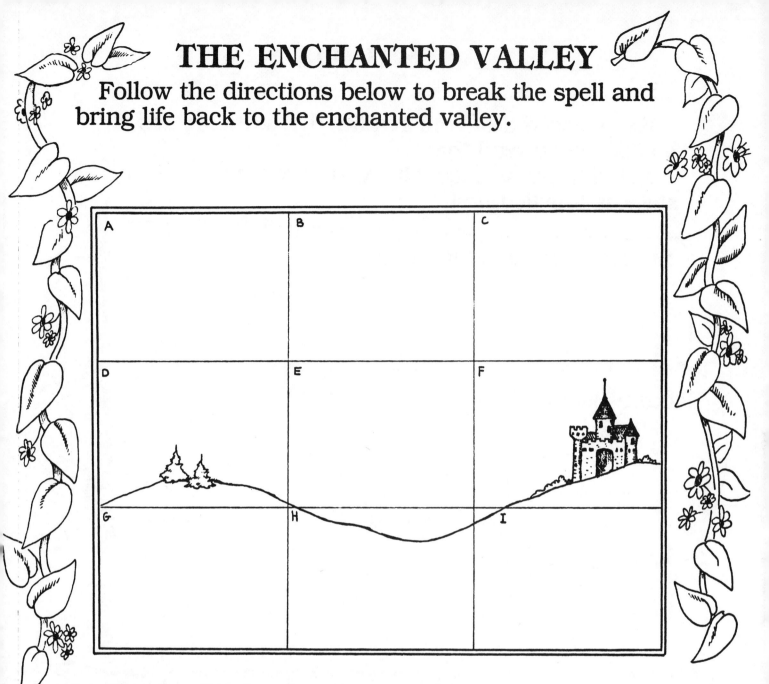

1. Draw a big bright sun in grid B.
2. Draw 2 birds in flight in grid F.
3. Put a small boat in the center of grid G.
4. Draw a puffy cloud in grid E and another in grid C.
5. Draw a lake in grid G and make it go into half of grid H.
6. Put 3 more trees in grid D.
7. Fill grid I with pretty little meadow flowers.
8. Fly a flag from the castle.
9. Bring it all to life by coloring it!

_____ 'S BOOK STACK

Keep a record of your reading by writing titles of books as you read them.

Ask a friend to race with you to see whose book stack is finished first.

Stories from Real Life

Picture Book

Book about Animals

Poetry

Fairy Tale Book

ANIMAL NOTES

Select an animal that you would like to know more about.

Use 2 books from the library to help you learn more about this animal.

Make notes below and share your information with your teacher or parent.

Name of animal _____

Titles of books   1.   _____
                   2.   _____

Description of animal _____

_____

_____

Where the animal lives _____

How the animal looks _____

What the animal eats _____

Other interesting facts

_____

_____

_____

_____

THE MAGIC KINGDOM OF READING

Read one book about each subject listed on the signs pointing to the Magic Kingdom of Reading.

Write the full title of the book you read on each sign.

When all the signs are filled, color the picture.

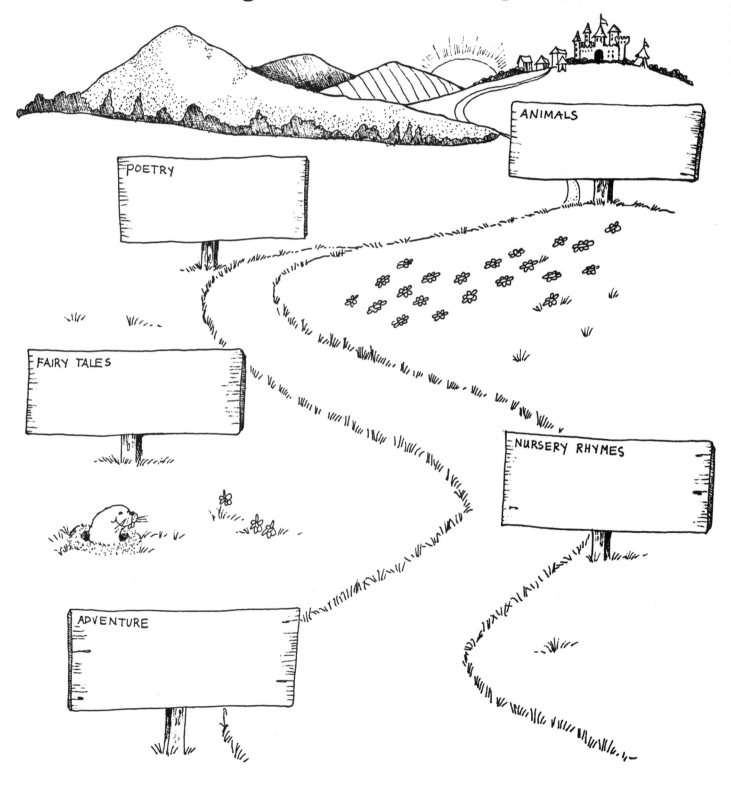

A LETTER TO THE AUTHOR

Select a book that you like.
Write a letter to the author.
Tell the author the name of the book you have selected, what you like about the book, and how you would have changed it if <u>you</u> had been the author.
Share your letter with your teacher or librarian.

Dear _____ ,

Sincerely,

READ AWAY!

Open any of these books and get ready to "read away" to a world of adventure.

Check the books you have already read, and use this stack as your personal library guide.

The Violet Fairy Book — ANDREW LANG

STORIES FROM AFRICA — Marguerite Dolch

Norwegian Folk Tales — by P.C. Asbjornsen

MONSTER GALLERY — LEAH WASKEY

The Story of Dragons — THOMAS AYLESWORTH

Pebbles from a Broken Jar — by Frances Alexander

A Book of Mermaids — Ruth Manning-Sanders

LEGENDARY AUSTRALIAN TALES — by Mrs. Langloh Parker

The Caldecott Aesop — Randolph Caldecott

The TROLL Book — by Michael Berenstain

TALES FROM A TAIWAN KITCHEN — by CORA CHENEY

GIANTS & GNOMES — by LANA SLATON

ANSWER KEY

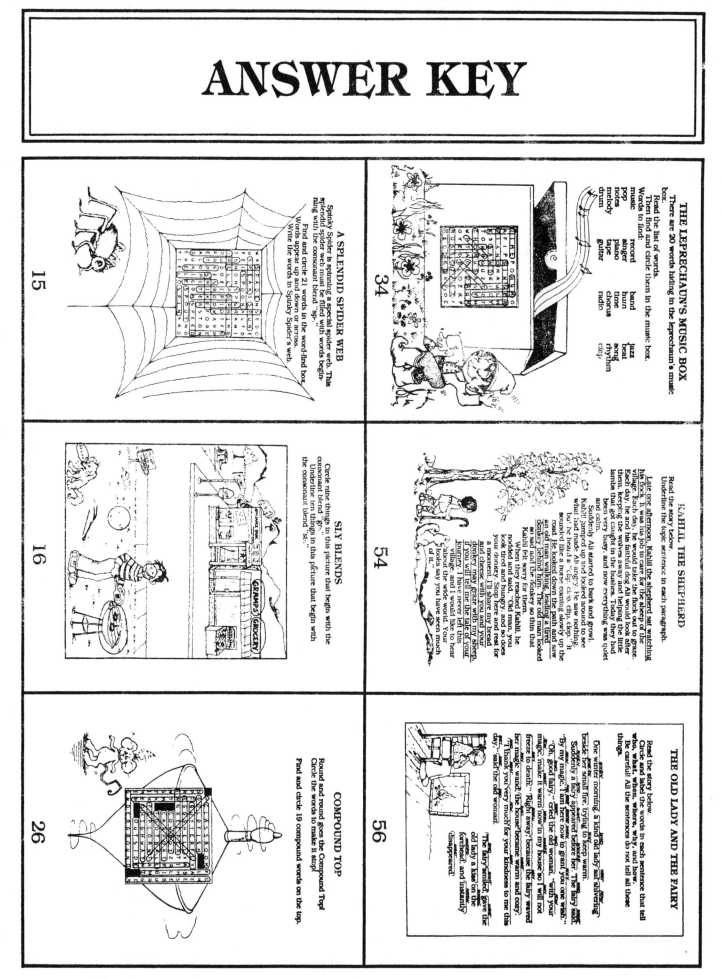

THE LEPRECHAUN'S MUSIC BOX

There are 20 words hiding in the leprechaun's music box.
Read the list of words.
Then find and circle them in the music box.
Words to find:

music	record	band	jazz
pop	singer	hum	beat
notes	piano	time	song
melody	tape	chorus	rhythm
drum	guitar	radio	clap

34

KAHLIL THE SHEPHERD

Read the story below.
Underline the topic sentence in each paragraph.

Late one afternoon, Kahlil the shepherd sat watching his flock. It was his job to care for the sheep of the village. Each day, he would take the flock out to graze. Each day, he and his faithful dog Ali would look after them, keeping the wolves away and helping the little lambs that got caught in the bushes. Today they had been very busy, and now everything was quiet and calm.

Suddenly Ali started to bark and growl. Kahlil jumped up and looked around to see what had made Ali angry. He saw nothing, but he heard a "clip, clop, clip, clop." It sounded like a horse coming slowly up the road. He looked down the path and saw an old man walking, leading a tired donkey behind him. The old man looked so sad and the donkey so thin that Kahlil felt sorry for them.

When they reached Kahlil, he nodded and said, "Old man, you look tired and hungry, and so does your donkey. Stop here and rest for a moment. I'll share my bread and cheese with you and your donkey may graze with my sheep. If you will tell me the tale of your journey. I have never left this village, and I would like to hear about the wide world. Your looks say you have seen much of it."

54

THE OLD LADY AND THE FAIRY

Read the story below.
Circle and label the words in each sentence that tell who, what, when, where, why, and how.
Be careful! All the sentences do not tell all these things.

One winter morning, a kind old lady sat shivering beside her small fire, trying to keep warm.

Suddenly a fairy appeared before her. The fairy said, "By my magic, I am here now to grant you one wish."

"Oh, good fairy," cried the old woman, "with your magic, make it warm now in my house so I will not freeze to death."

"Right away! because the fairy waved her magic wand, the house became warm and cozy.

"Thank you very much for your kindness to me this day," said the old woman.

The fairy smiled, gave the old lady a kiss on the forehead, and instantly disappeared.

56

A SPLENDID SPIDER WEB

Spinky Spider is spinning a special spider web. This splendid spider web must be filled with words beginning with the consonant blend "sp."
Find and circle 21 words in the word-find box. Words appear up and down or across.
Write the words in Spinky Spider's web.

15

SLY BLENDS

Circle nine things in this picture that begin with the consonant blend "gr."
Underline ten things in this picture that begin with the consonant blend "st."

16

COMPOUND TOP

Round and round goes the Compound Top!
Circle the words to make it stop!
Find and circle 19 compound words on the top.

26

79

Adventure lasts a lifetime if
You're willing to pursue
Each newly opened book to bring
The Unicorn to you!